# Simply ORGANIZED

EMILIE BARNES

**HARVEST HOUSE PUBLISHERS**
Eugene, Oregon 97402

Dost thou love life?
Then do not squander time,
for that is the stuff life is made of.

—Ben Franklin

# Me, Get Organized?

Over the years I have received countless letters from women who want to know how to get organized. Whether married or single, working or staying at home, women all across the country have realized how much more effective they could be if they somehow could get organized.

That word *organized* means many things to many people, however. For some it might be putting papers in colored file folders; for others it means putting all their seasonings in alphabetical order. For some it means a clean house, and for others, being able to retrieve papers that have been stored away.

Even after writing 26 books with a combined total of over 6,000 pages dealing with this topic, I'm not sure I have covered all bases for all women. I have found, though, the following basic steps to be extremely helpful when a person wants to become organized.

✍♥ *Start with you.* What is it about you that causes you to be disorganized? I find that organized people have a calmness and serenity about them that disorganized people don't have. Search your own self to see what is causing all that confusion. Get rid of that clutter first before you move on.

- *Keep it simple.* There are many programs available, but choose one that's simple. You don't want to spend all your time keeping up charts and graphs.

- *Make sure everything has a designated place.* One of my sayings is "Don't put it down, put it away." Another, "Don't pile it, file it." If there is no place for stuff to go, it's going to get piled. And that's one thing you want to prevent—piles.

- *Store like items together.* My husband, Bob, has his gardening supplies and tools together. I have my laundry items in one place, my bill-paying tools in one area, my cups/saucers, my drinking glasses, and my dinnerware all in their general area. Don't spend time going from here to there getting ready for your tasks. Put like items in one place.

- *Even though you are neat, you may not be organized.* I tell women to use notebook organizers and that there are two things to remember. One, write it down; and two, read it. It doesn't do you much good to write down that birthday date or crucial appointment on your calendar and forget both because you didn't read your calendar. Remember to write and read.

- *Get rid of all items you don't use.* They only add to the clutter.

- *Invest in the proper tools.* In order to be organized you need proper tools: bins, hooks, racks, containers, lazy Susans, etc.

- *Involve the whole family.* Learn to delegate jobs and responsibilities to other members of the family. My Bob takes care of all the repairs. When something is broken, he is Mr. Fix-It. Tailor chores to fit the ages of your children. Also, change off frequently so no one gets bored. Most importantly, don't do something yourself that another member of the family can do.

- *Keep master lists.* I've learned to use a three-ring binder, 3" x 5" file cards, and journals to keep track of all our stuff. You may think you'll never forget you loaned that CD to Brad or that video to Christine, but you will. Write it down and keep the list in a place where you cannot overlook it.

- *Use a lot of labels and signs.* If containers, bins, drawers, and shelves aren't labeled, the family won't be able to spot where things go. I have also used color coding to help identify items belonging to various members of the family: blue for Bevan, red for Chad, and purple for Christine. I use a permanent fine-point paint pen very effectively to label clothes, glass and plastic jars, and wooden items.

- *Continually reevaluate your system.* Nothing is written in concrete. It can be changed. See how other people do things, read a book to gather ideas, evaluate your own system. Change when it's not working.


Where to start? Start with these suggestions. Once you have them under control, you're ready for more specific areas. And the first specific area we're going to start with is *you.*

# Simply Organized . . .

# For You

He who every morning plans the transaction of the day and follows out that plan carries a thread that will guide him through the labyrinth of the most busy life . . . But where no plan is laid . . . chaos will soon reign.

—Victor Hugo

# How to Feel Personally Organized

D o you ever look around your home, room, or office and just want to throw up your hands in disgust and say, "It's no use. I'll never get organized!" You need not feel that way anymore. With a few simple tools you can feel personally organized.

The old saying, "Everything has a place and everything is in its place," is very helpful to keep in mind. To help you accomplish this you need four tools:

✍ A "To Do" list

✍ A calendar

✍ A telephone/address source list

✍ A simple filing system

These four tools can drastically change your life from feeling confused to feeling organized.

## A "To Do" List

Have the first three of these tools be the same size (8-1/2" x 11"; 8-1/2" x 5-1/2"; etc.). This way you won't have to fight with different sizes of paper.

After arriving at your size of paper, write with a regular ink pen the words "To Do" at the top of the page, and begin writing down all the things that are in your head you need to do. As you accomplish each item, you will get so much pleasure in crossing off what's been done. At the end of each day, review your list and update any new things you need to add to your list. At the end of the week consolidate your pages for the week and start again on Monday with a fresh page. As you get more experienced with this list, you will want to rank items by importance. This added technique will help you maximize your time.

## A Calendar

I recommend three types of calendars, the first being a two-page month-at-a-glance calendar. At one glance you get a good overview of the month. Details aren't written here, but you do jot down broad descriptions of engagements with times—for example, meetings, lunches, dinners, parties, dentist appointments, etc. The second type of calendar shows an entire week on a two-page format. *The Daily Planner* (Harvest House Publishers) also includes a small calendar for the month and room for notes on each week's section. The third type of calendar has a page for each day. On this day-at-a-glance calendar you get more detailed and specific and jot down what you will be doing for each hour or half hour.

## A Telephone/Address Source List

This listing becomes your personal telephone and address book. (Many daily planners have a place for a list like this.) In this book you design your own directory of information that you will use for home, work, or play. You might want to list certain numbers by broad headings such as: schools, attorneys, dentists, doctors, plumbers, carpenters, restaurants, etc. Broad headings help in looking up the specifics when you can't remember the person's last name.

## A Simple Filing System

Adopt this motto: "Don't pile it, file it." This principle will really tidy your area up. Go to your local stationery store and purchase about four dozen 8-1/2" x 14" colored or manila file folders. I recommend colored file folders because they are brighter and add a little cheer to your day. I find that the legal size (8-1/2" x 14") folders are more functional—they can accommodate the longer-sized papers.

On these folders, use simple headings for each: Sales Tax, Auto, Insurance, School Papers, Maps, Warranties, Taxes, Checks, etc. Then take all those loose papers you find around your home and put them in their proper place. Remember: "Don't pile it, file it." If you have a metal file drawer to house these folders, that's great. If not, just pick up a cardboard storage box (the "Perfect Box" with a lid, see page 19) to get started. Later you can move up to a better file cabinet.

Don't you already feel some relief by just reading about these four aids? I hope you do!

Whatever your hand finds to do,
do it with all your might.

—*The Book of Ecclesiastes*

# A Purse that Works

Pete has just returned with the babysitter, and you're running late for that long-anticipated class reunion. But you want everything to be perfect.

Julie has spilled the cat's milk dish and you're sticking to the kitchen floor, trying to clean up the mess. The phone rings and the rollers are falling out of your hair. "Time—I need more time!" you yell. Pete takes over the cleanup. Your sitter holds baby Jason, and you put Julie in her rocker with a book.

Now it's time for you. Grabbing the cute clutch that matches your outfit, you begin to change purses. As you try to decide what to take out of your everyday bag you begin to wade through the papers, gum wrappers, pacifiers, etc., that have collected in the bottom of your bag. This only gets you upset and frustrated. Dumping the whole contents of the purse on the bed, you say, "Forget it!" Because you're running late, you end up taking your crummy tote bag—which doesn't match your lovely outfit in the least.

End your purse frustrations once and for all. Using these few simple steps, you will be able to change bags and do it quickly. You will never need to hassle with purse-changing again!

# Getting Started

What you'll need is a nice-sized purse for everyday use. Then you'll need three to seven little bags. They can be made of quilted fabric (with zipper or Velcro fasteners) or of denim or corduroy prints. Make each little bag different in color and size to identify it more easily. (These little bags can also be purchased.) Your everyday handbag should be pretty good-sized, since it's the one you'll be dragging around with you (and your kids) all over the place. It should be able to hold everything that you'll need.

# The Wallet

Find a wallet that's functional for you, because a wallet is very, very important. You want a wallet that has a section where you can keep a few bills and a zipper compartment for change. Keep your most frequently used credit cards, your checkbook, your driver's license, and all those other little important things in your wallet. (You should also keep a pen with your wallet.) Now when you run to the cleaner or the pharmacy to pick something up, rather than taking your big purse with everything in it, all you have to do is pull your wallet out of your purse, run in, and make your little exchange.

# The Little Bags

In the little bags you'll keep all sorts of things. One bag holds my sunglasses. In my makeup bags I keep such things as a mirror, lipstick, a small comb, blush, nail clippers, nail file, etc. I also keep some change for an emergency phone call.

In addition to my wallet, sunglasses bag, and makeup bag, I have a bag for reading glasses and two more small bags for various items.

# Everything Organized

Suppose your good friend Sue calls you and asks you to lunch. If you decide to go, you can just grab your clutch purse and put a few of the little bags in it. For example, you'll want to take your wallet and credit cards plus your makeup bags. How long will this take you? Not even a minute. You just stick your purse under your arm, and you're off. When you come home again, just take out the little bags and put them back into your everyday purse.

# Items for Your Purse

A.  Wallet:
    pen, checkbook                  driver's license
    change compartment              calendar (current)
    money, credit cards             pictures (most used)

B.  Makeup Bag 1:
    lipstick, blush                 mirror
    comb, small brush               telephone change

C.  Makeup Bag 2:
    breath mints, gum, cough drops  scissors (small)
    small perfume                   Kleenex
    hand cream                      nail file
    nail clippers                   matches

D.  Eyeglass case for sunglasses

E.  Eyeglass case for reading, spare glasses

F.  Small Bag 1:
    business cards (yours and
    your husband's) for:
    • hairdresser                   • seldom-used credit cards
    • doctor (health plan)          • tea bag, Sweet 'n' Low, aspirin

- insurance person
- auto club
- library card
- small calculator

G.  Small Bag 2:
    small Bible, paperback book
    needle, thread, pins, thimble
    Band-Aid
    collapsible cup
    tape measure

    toothbrush
    toothpicks
    spot remover
    feminine protection

*Well done is better than well said.*

*—Ben Franklin*

# Wardrobe Wonders

**N**ow let's get into our closet and get organized. Let's weed out some of those things we don't need and get our closets in order.

## Getting Started

First, we need to get our equipment together. You'll need three trash bags (I suggest using black trash bags so you or your family cannot see what's inside them) and six to twelve boxes which are approximately 16" deep x 12" wide x 10" high with lids. I call these "Perfect Boxes." You'll also need a 3" x 5" card-file box with tabbed dividers and 3" x 5" colored index cards.

Now we're ready to get going! Label the trash bags "Put Away," "Give Away," and "Throw Away." Walk into the closet and take everything out.

As you pull items out of your closet, keep in mind that if you haven't worn it for the past year it goes in one of those three bags. Either you're going to put it away somewhere else, or you're going to give it away to somebody else, or you're going to throw it away. If you haven't worn it for two or three years, you'll definitely have to give it away or throw it away.

*EQUIPMENT YOU'LL NEED*

• *3 trash bags*

• *6 to 12 Perfect Boxes*

• *3" x 5" card file box with tabbed dividers*

• *3" x 5" colored index cards*

# Taking Inventory

Now let's start taking inventory. (You can use the Wardrobe Inventory sheet printed below.) As you begin to take your inventory, you'll quickly begin to see what you have and need. For example, you may have way too many pairs of navy-blue pants. You only need one pair of good navy-blue pants and maybe a couple pairs of nice jeans. You can begin to see where you've made your mistakes as you take your wardrobe inventory, and you'll be able to start correcting those mistakes.

## ❧ Wardrobe Inventory ❧

| BLOUSES | PANTS | SKIRTS |
|---------|-------|--------|
| JACKETS | SWEATERS | DRESSES |
| GOWNS | LINGERIE | SHOES |
| JEWELRY | | |

THINGS I NEED

# Everything in Its Place

Hang your things up as you put them back into your closet. Each thing should have a definite place. For example, all the extra hangers can go at the left end of your closet. Then arrange all your blouses according to color, then your pants, then your skirts, etc. If you have a jacket that matches your pants, separate them. (Hang the jacket with the jackets and the pants with the pants.)

This way you can mix or match your things and not always wear the same jacket and pants together.

Suggested order for your clothes:

1) Extra hangers

2) Blouses

3) Pants

4) Skirts

5) Blazers and jackets

6) Sweaters (these can also be folded and put on a shelf or in a drawer)

7) Dresses

Your shoes can go on shoe racks. Some neat different kinds of shoe racks are now available, or you can cover shoeboxes with wallpaper or Christmas paper. (Your children can help you do this.)

Your smaller handbags can go in clear plastic boxes. The larger ones can go up on the shelf above your wardrobe. A hanging plastic shoe bag is great because you can also put your purses and scarves in it. Belts and ties should go on hooks. Or you can just hammer a big nail into the wall. You'd be surprised at how many belts you can get on a nail!

## Storage—Put Away Boxes

Get your Perfect Boxes with lids and number each box. Assign each box a 3" x 5" card with a corresponding number. For example:

Box 1—Jenny's summer shorts, T-shirts, skirts, sandals

Box 2—Costume clothing: 1950s outfit, black-and-white saddle shoes, purple angora sweater with holes, high school cheerleader's outfit

Box 3—Ski clothes, socks, long underwear, sweaters, pants

Box 4—Scarves, belts, jewelry, honeymoon peignoir, etc.

File your 3" x 5" cards in their file box behind a tabbed divider marked "Storage." Now, when you want to find your stored ski clothes, you look through your card file and see that they're located in Box 3. What could be easier?

## Give Away

Be sure you give away things you're not using. Many people today have limited finances and can't afford some things. If you have clothes that you aren't wearing, give them to someone who will be able to use them. They'll be grateful to you, and you'll feel good about your giving.

## Throw Away

Put these items in a trash bag with a twistie on it and set out for the trash.

Now that you've got a good start on feeling personally organized, let's move on to your home. Keep your momentum going and forge ahead.

*Nothing is particularly hard
if you divide it into small jobs.*

—Henry Ford

# Total Mess to Total Rest

S uppose I were to say to you, "Today, I'm going to come home with you. I want you to take me into your house, and I want to go through your closets, to look under your bed, to open your drawers, to look in your pantry, and to go anyplace in your house. I just want to check out your house really well."

Some of you would reply, "Well, that's okay. I've got my house in order, and things are really good there, so you can come over." Others of you would say, "Okay, but don't go into the third bedroom. I've been shoving things in that back bedroom for a long time." Still others of you might say, "There is no way anybody is going to come into my house, because the whole place is a total mess."

## Controlling Your Home

I am going to show you how to take that mess, no matter what size it is, and turn it into a home that you'll be able to maintain and rest in. You will control your home instead of your home controlling you.

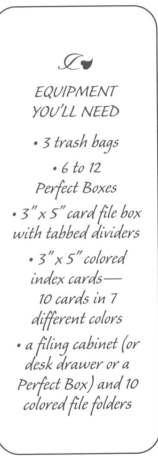

**EQUIPMENT YOU'LL NEED**

• 3 trash bags

• 6 to 12 Perfect Boxes

• 3" x 5" card file box with tabbed dividers

• 3" x 5" colored index cards— 10 cards in 7 different colors

• a filing cabinet (or desk drawer or a Perfect Box) and 10 colored file folders

We're going to use the same principles we used on your closet, so you've already had some practice.

You'll want to commit yourself to five weeks to unclutter your clutter. I don't want you to become overwhelmed thinking about it, because you're going to take a small portion at a time—only one room a week for the next five weeks. You'll do it nice and slow, so that you'll gradually get your home organized.

It can all be done in 15-minute time slots. On Monday, go into Room 1 and clean like mad for 15 minutes, then forget it until Tuesday and do the same as you did Monday, spending 15 minutes cleaning and organizing. Continue this process throughout the week. Presto! By the end of the week you will have spent one hour and 30 minutes in Room 1. You'll still have Sunday off and a nice, clean, well-organized room. Continue this process until every room in the house is complete.

So start with three large trash bags and label them "Put Away," "Throw Away," and "Give Away." Now visualize yourself standing at the front door with these three big trash bags. Ring the doorbell, then walk through the front door. The first room you come to will be the first room you're going to clean, with the exception of the kitchen. (If that's the room you walk into first, move on. Save the kitchen, because you'll need all the experience you can get before tackling it.) To make it easy, let's say we step into the living room, and on our right is the hall closet.

So we open up the hall closet. We're now going to take everything out of that hall closet. We have to decide to get vicious in making choices about what to do with all the stuff we've taken out of the hall closet. I recommend that you call a friend who would like to help you with your house (and you help with her house). It's great to have a friend because she'll help you make decisions that you haven't been able to make for 15 years.

## The Hall Closet

Let's put into the hall closet all those things that actually belong in a hall closet. These include sweaters, coats, umbrella, books, football blanket, binoculars, tennis rackets, etc.

But now we have all these other things that don't belong in there, such as old magazines we've collected for six or seven years. (We were going to look through them some rainy day and cut out the pictures and recipes, but we never did.) So we have to get rid of these things. We've also got papers and receipts and all sorts of other things in that hall closet, so we'll put these either in the Put Away bag, the Throw Away bag, or the Give Away bag.

As we go through our home every week for the next five weeks, we begin to

fill up these bags. At the end of the fifth week we may have three, ten, or fifteen bags full of various things. Then we put twisties on the trash bags marked Throw Away and set them out for the trashman. Now they're gone! You've got all those things out of the way.

Now you have two types of bags left: the Give Away bags and the Put Away bags. The Give Away bags will hold things that you may want to hand down to some other family member or to relatives, or clothing that you want to give to a thrift shop, sell at a garage or rummage sale, or donate to your church. And what do you do with the contents of the Put Away bags? Either put the items in their place in the house, or place them in one of your Perfect Boxes. Be sure to note box number and contents on your index filecard.

27

# Keeping It Organized

We have our house totally clean. How are we going to maintain it that way? We certainly never want to go through this clutter again! You'll be glad to know we won't have to do it again.

Take your 3" x 5" cards and tabbed dividers. Label the dividers with the following (you already have the "Storage" divider if you went through your wardrobe in the last chapter):

| | |
|---|---|
| —Daily | —Biannually |
| —Weekly | —Annually |
| —Monthly | —Storage |
| —Quarterly | |

Assign a color of index cards to each section. On the first set of cards, list those jobs you do daily, such as washing the dishes, making the bed, and picking up around the house. On the next set of cards, list your weekly chores; on the next set, your monthly chores, and so on. Below I've made suggestions for dividing the household tasks.

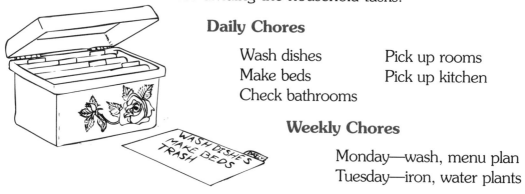

## Daily Chores

Wash dishes     Pick up rooms
Make beds     Pick up kitchen
Check bathrooms

## Weekly Chores

Monday—wash, menu plan
Tuesday—iron, water plants

Wednesday—mop floors

Thursday—vacuum, grocery shop

Friday—change bed linens, dust

Saturday—yard work

Sunday—free (except plan for next week!)

## Monthly Chores

Week 1—clean refrigerator

Week 2—clean oven

Week 3—wax furniture

Week 4—clean and dust baseboards

## Quarterly Chores

Straighten drawers

Clean windows

Clean closets

Move furniture and vacuum

Dust and straighten china cabinets

Clean cupboards

Clean mini-blinds

## Biannual Chores

Clean screens

Rearrange furniture

## Annual Chores

Wash curtains

Clean carpets

Prune trees

Clean drapes

Clean out garage/basement/attic

Now let's say Thursday comes along and your good friend Sue calls and says, "Let's go to lunch, then do some shopping. The department store has a big sale today." So you check your cards and say, "I've done all my daily things, but it's Thursday, so I have to vacuum and go to the market. I can do my marketing this afternoon when we get back, but I don't know about the vacuuming."

You move the vacumming to Friday, but there's already a list of things to do. So you move those chores to Saturday, but you promised the kids you'd take them to the park. But moving the chores to Sunday isn't going to work either, because you have company coming over after church! By Monday morning you have a million things to do, and the house is already starting to look messy again.

So, you're not going to move the vacuuming to Friday. Instead, you're going to move it to the back of the weekly section. That's right—you're not going to vacuum again until next Thursday, when the vacuuming card comes up again in the file. Rotate the cards daily, whether you do the allotted jobs or not.

By following this system, you avoid cramming a week's worth of housekeeping chores into one day, *and* you develop a routine that helps keep your priorities in order. When Sue calls next Thursday and invites you to lunch and shopping, you take a look at your unvacuumed floor and say, "How about I meet you at the mall after lunch? I've got a couple of things I need to finish up around here."

*If you miss a job on an allotted day, skip it. Put the card in back of the file, and do the chore next week.*

Next you have your monthly chores. During Week 1 you clean the refrigerator (you have a whole week to do it, or you can delegate the job to a child). During Week 2 you do the oven, and so forth. This way, every week you're doing a little bit to maintain your home. It's only going to take you a little time, but you're continually maintaining your home so you never have to go through that total mess program again. Next you have your quarterly things to do (straighten drawers, etc.). Then you have your semiannual tasks (rearrange furniture, wash curtains, etc.). Finally, there are the annual jobs such as cleaning the basement, attic, garage, etc.

Your last tab, at the very back of your file, is your storage tab, which we started when we sorted through the wardrobe. Your 3" x 5" cards are numbered Box 1, Box 2, Box 3, and Perfect Boxes are given a corresponding number. If you want to go a step further, you can make out two cards for each box—one to be pasted on the box and one to go into your card file. Items in your Put Away bags that need to be stored go in these boxes.

Now we take our file box and our colored file folders and look at what's left in our Put Away bags. What do we find? We find old newspaper clippings, warranties, instruction booklets, receipts from car repairs and household repairs, and all kinds of other things. So we put these papers in our colored file folders, label the folders (see the suggested list below), list all those things on 3" x 5" cards, and file the cards away under "Storage" in our file box.

### Suggested Labels for Colored File Folders

—Medical
—Warranties
—Insurance papers and booklets
—Car repair receipts

—Appliance instructions
—Decorating ideas
—Special notes, letters, cards
—Receipts from major purchases

What have we done? We've taken a big step toward simply organizing our house—and maintaining that organization. What does that give us? More hours in our day, with no guilt feelings about a cluttered house.

# Speed Cleaning

Here are some helpful tips to make your cleaning go as quickly and smoothly as possible.

1. *Have a good set of cleaning tools on hand.* First-class tools make you feel like you're doing a first-class job. A few items everyone should have:

   - apron
   - feather duster—Invest in an ostrich duster. These are super for moving small amounts of dust from higher levels to lower levels. Use fast but smooth strokes. When finished, shake the duster outside to remove dust from the feathers.
   - pumice stone—Get that ugly ring out of the toilet caused by rust and mineral deposits! It's amazing how fast it will remove the scale. Just rub it on the ring and slosh with water as you rub. Pumice also cleans ovens and removes the carbon build-up on grills and iron cookware.
   - knee pads—Billy's old football knee pads are great protectors for cleaning floors and tubs.
   - toothbrush—to clean the hard corners of areas on floors, showers, and around faucets.
   - whisk broom
   - window/mirror cleaner
   - cloth baby diaper—for cleaning windows
   - all-purpose cleaner
   - dish cloth—for wet cleaning. Use 100 percent cotton cloths.
   - ammonia—excellent cleaner (not the sudsy type) for floors.
   - oven cleaner
   - rubber gloves

2. *Always start at the top of the room, work down and around.* Mop or vacuum last.

3. *Go in one direction.* Work around your room from top to bottom and from right to left (or left to right). Always start at one end of your home and work toward the other end. Don't get sidetracked with this mess and that mess.
4. *Put on some music with a very fast beat.* This will help your cleaning go faster plus take your mind off the drudgery.
5. *Work in 15-minute increments.* Set your kitchen timer for 15 minutes and work like crazy until it goes off. You'll be surprised at how much you can accomplish!
6. *Try to avoid interruptions.* Let the answering machine take phone messages and call back when it's convenient.
7. *Use these speed-cleaning tips.*

   - Before cleaning window panes, wipe or vacuum sills and wood cross frames. With your window cleaner and baby diaper, use a horizontal stroke on the outside and a vertical stroke on the inside. If you miss a spot, you'll be able to tell which side of the window it's on.
   - Use your feather duster to dusk silk flowers, soft fabric items, plants, picture frames, lampshades, windowsills, bookshelves, and door frames. (Since you're working top to bottom, you'll be vacuuming up this dust soon.)
   - After wiping your wastebaskets clean, give the inside bottom a quick coat of floor wax. This will prevent trash from sticking to the bottom of the wastebasket in the future.
   - Change your air conditioner and heater filters every six months, and wipe off the blades of your window and/or room fans quarterly. This will keep the dust and dirt from circulating through your rooms.

8. *Make big tasks into smaller tasks.* If cleaning the refrigerator seems overwhelming, clean the bottom shelf on Monday, the middle shelf on Tuesday, the fruit and vegetable drawers on Wednesday, and the outside on Thursday. Big projects become more manageable when broken into smaller parts.
9. *Don't forget to treat yourself for a job well done.* After you finish a task, enjoy a cup of coffee or tea, or put on a face masque and take a hot bath— whatever you find rewarding for your labors!

# Getting Your Kitchen Under Control

Do you realize that one of the reasons you're desperate for kitchen organization is because you spend an average of 1,092 hours a year in the kitchen? That's a lot of hours in an area that definitely needs to be organized.

## Getting Started

First you'll need some jars. Tupperware is a wonderful thing to have as well. Those lazy Susan turntables are also super. Also get Contact paper, newspapers, or anything that you can cover some boxes with. You'll also need trash bags, plus a felt-tip marker pen and some labels.

## Scheduling Time

The next crucial thing is to schedule a time. Here's what I recommend: Set the timer on your stove for 15 minutes, then work like mad until the timer goes off. Then do whatever else you have to. If

*EQUIPMENT YOU'LL NEED*

- *jars*
- *Tupperware*
- *lazy Susans*
- *Perfect Boxes labeled "Kitchen Overflow"*
- *Contact paper to match the colors of your kitchen*
- *trash bags marked "Throw Away" and "Give Away"*
- *felt-tip pen*
- *labels*

35

you're working toward a deadline, you have a tendency to move a little faster. So schedule yourself a time in the day when you're going to organize your kitchen.

## First Stop: the Cupboards

First, let's open all cupboard doors. Starting with the cupboards closest to the sink (because these are the ones we get in and out of the most and that are probably in the biggest mess), pull *everything* out. Wipe out the shelves and repaper with Contact paper if needed.

Now for the things you're not using, such as broken dishes, mugs, vases, plus cleansers and other things that are partially used but you'll never use again. Put these in either your Throw Away bag, your Give Away bag, or a Perfect Box marked "Kitchen Overflow." These seldom-used boxes can be stored on the garage shelves or where you have extra room.

The things you don't use very often should go back in the cup-boards, but on the highest shelves. This might include such things as big platters for your Thanksgiving turkey. (You might use this only once or twice a year.)

*Glue a 12-inch square of cork to the inside of the cabinet door over your kitchen work area. On the cork tack the recipe card you are using and newspaper clippings of recipes you plan to try within a few days. It keeps them at eye level, and they stay spatter-free.*

Items that you use daily go back into the cupboards in easily accessible places. Such things as spices, dishes, pots and pans, etc., should be put back neatly. I use lazy Susan turntables for my spices, or you can use a spice rack. (A spice rack or a lazy Susan also comes in handy for vitamin bottles.)

Get your broken appliances repaired. They're sitting around waiting for somebody to pay attention to them. Those that would cost more than half the cost of a new appliance to repair should be thrown out.

For those of you who have high school students going to college, put your extra appliances in a box and store them away. When our children went off to college and started getting their own apartments, they wanted such things as the extra iron, toaster, etc. So label them and number them. Then put this information in your card files.

*Mark your storage bowls and their covers with the same number, using a marking pencil. Then you won't always be looking for a matching cover for the bowl when you're putting away leftovers. All you have to do is match the numbers.*

## Kitchen Overflow

Now for your overflow. At one time Bob and I and the children lived in a condominium. We had moved from a big two-story house to a small three-bedroom condominium. I found that when I was organizing the kitchen I didn't have a place for everything. That's when I discovered what I call the kitchen overflow. If you're lucky enough to have a shelf or cabinets in the garage, that's a good place to put the overflow. If not, get some boxes with lids and put the overflow in them. The overflow might include such things as a waffle iron, an extra set of dishes, or even extra canned goods.

What can you do with gadgets and utensils if you're short on space? Put them in a crock and tie a little bow around it. The crock looks cute on the counter, and all your whips and wooden spoons and spatulas can probably fit in it. Set the crock close to the stove or at some other handy spot.

## Unavoidable Junk

Then there are the junk drawers. There is no way to eliminate these, so don't feel you have to get rid of those junk drawers. We all have them. The problem is, they are usually very junky. But we can take that junk and pretty well clean it up. My junk drawer has a little silverware sectional container. In it I put the hammer, the screwdriver, and a couple of those small artichoke jars in which I keep some cup hooks, nails, screws, and thumbtacks—all those little things. You may want to get two or three jars to put in your junk drawer so you'll have everything fairly organized when you pull it out.

Another handy organizer is an egg carton. This is fabulous to use for those little screws. You can cut apart the cartons so that you have small sections of egg cartons. Then the screws, hooks, etc., can fit in there and go nicely in your junk drawer.

# Pantry Space

Even if you don't have a pantry, you may have a cupboard in your kitchen that you're using as a pantry. The pantry can be organized in a really fun and cute way. Organize your staples and canned goods by category. For example, put canned fruit in one row and dry cereal in another. To help keep your food items in the right place, label your pantry shelves accordingly.

Put packaged items, such as dried taco mix, salad dressings, gravies, etc., into a large jar or small shoebox covered with wallpaper or contact paper. You can also purchase plastic or metal sliding shelves.

Put everything you can in jars—rice, Bisquick, popcorn, beans, sugar, flour, graham crackers, cookies, raisins, coffee filters, dog biscuits.

As you plan your weekly menus, check your staple and perishable foods and replenish if necessary.

## ✒♥ Pantry Stocking List ✒♥

Date_____

| Qty. | Cost | STARCHES | Qty. | Cost | CANNED & BOTTLED GOODS | Qty. | Cost | |
|---|---|---|---|---|---|---|---|---|
| ___ | ___ | Flour | ___ | ___ | Tuna | ___ | ___ | Brown Mustard |
| ___ | ___ | Cornmeal | ___ | ___ | Juices | ___ | ___ | Yellow Mustard |
| ___ | ___ | Oatmeal | ___ | ___ | Peanut Butter | ___ | ___ | Oil |
| ___ | ___ | Pasta | ___ | ___ | Tomato Sauce | ___ | ___ | Tabasco Sauce |
| ___ | ___ | White Rice | ___ | ___ | Tomato Paste | | | Worcestershire |
| ___ | ___ | Brown Rice | ___ | ___ | Dried Fruit | | | Sauce |
| ___ | ___ | Potatoes | ___ | ___ | Dried Mixes | | | |
| | | | | | (i.e. Salad Dressing, Taco Mix) | | | PERISHABLE FOODS |
| ___ | ___ | | ___ | ___ | Canned Vegetables | ___ | ___ | Fresh Garlic |
| | | | ___ | ___ | Canned Fruit | ___ | ___ | Ginger |
| | | SWEET-BASED STAPLES | ___ | ___ | Pancake Mix | ___ | ___ | Green Peppers |
| ___ | ___ | Brown Sugar | ___ | ___ | Jello | ___ | ___ | Celery |
| ___ | ___ | White Sugar | ___ | ___ | Pudding Mix | ___ | ___ | Eggs |
| ___ | ___ | Powdered Sugar | ___ | ___ | Soup | ___ | ___ | Nuts |
| ___ | ___ | Honey | | | | ___ | ___ | Green Onions |
| ___ | ___ | Maple Syrup | | | | ___ | ___ | Yellow Onions |
| ___ | ___ | Jams/Jellies | | | | ___ | ___ | White Onions |
| | | | | | | ___ | ___ | Tomatoes |
| ___ | ___ | | | | | ___ | ___ | Carrots |
| | | | | | CONDIMENTS | ___ | ___ | White Cheese |
| | | | ___ | ___ | Catsup | ___ | ___ | Yellow Cheese |
| | | | ___ | ___ | Vinegar | ___ | ___ | Lemons |
| | | | ___ | ___ | Capers | | | |

## Work Together, Store Together

Things that work together should be stored together. What does this mean? If you're going to organize baking items—your mixing bowls, your hand mixer, your measuring cups—all those things can be stored in one small area together. I bake homemade bread, so I have on my shelf all those things that I use to bake the bread. I have my pans, the oil, the honey, the flour, the yeast, etc., handy, so that when I'm ready to bake bread I don't have to be running from cupboard  to cupboard trying to find things. Coffeepot, filters, coffee, and even mugs could also be stored together.

Put kitchen towels and cloths in a drawer or on a shelf close to the sink. Keep pot holders near point of use.

## Pots and Pans

Pots and pans should be kept neatly somewhere near the stove. You can line the shelves for the pots with plain or light-colored paper—maybe brown paper. Determine the best possible position for your pans, because those are things you use often and need to get out quickly. You can draw a circle or

square the size of the pan with a black felt pen, then write the pan size inside the circle or square. For example, here is where the nine-inch frying pan goes and that's where the two-quart saucepan goes. If you have people other than yourself doing things in your kitchen, this is a wonderful way for them to know where things are to be stored.

## The Refrigerator

What about the refrigerator? Look at that refrigerator as just another closet, because basically that's what it is—a cold-storage closet. Fruits and vegetables should be put in plastic containers with lids, plastic bags, or refrigerator drawers. Cheese and meats go on the coldest shelf. Use all types of see-through containers with tight lids.

Lazy Susans are great space-savers in your refrigerator. I have two of them. One is on the top shelf and stores the milk and the half-and-half. The other one has the sour cream, the cottage cheese, etc.

You can also buy dispensers and bottle racks for your refrigerator. Can dispensers are good if you use a lot of soft drinks. Some dispensers you can set right onto the shelf in your refrigerator, and they dispense from right there. There are also special milk dispensers, juice dispensers, and so forth. Your children will absolutely love these.

At least once a year pull the plug on your refrigerator and give it a thorough cleaning with baking soda (one tablespoon baking soda to one quart water). Let it air dry.

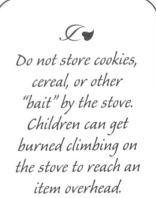

*Do not store cookies, cereal, or other "bait" by the stove. Children can get burned climbing on the stove to reach an item overhead.*

# The Freezer

Now what about the freezer? All your frozen vegetables should be put in one section and your meats in another section. All your casseroles that you premake can also be put together. When I make a lasagna casserole or spaghetti sauce, I make enough for that night plus one for the freezer. And I always label and date containers so I'll know how long they've been in the freezer. If you are freezing in jars, leave 1/2" at the top to allow for expansion.

I also try to keep emergency meals in the freezer in case company drops in or I've been too busy to prepare anything else. You can buy plastic containers especially for making TV dinners. With these, if you have leftovers from the meal, you can put together one TV dinner with foil around the top, then label it and put it into the freezer. When you get four or five of these accumulated, you've got a nice meal for everyone that's just a little different.

Be sure you label dishes that go into the freezer, because otherwise you'll find mystery packages in the freezer as you clean it out. It's amazing how things don't look the same when they're frozen!

Ice cream and frozen desserts should go together in your freezer. Did you know that you can freeze potato chips, corn chips, tortillas, muffins, and bread? If you use wheat flour, be sure to keep that in the freezer so it will keep nice and fresh. Candles should also be kept in the freezer. (If you keep them in the freezer, they won't drip or pop when you light them.)

# Kitchen Basics

No matter how large or small, any kitchen can be tailored to suit your lifestyle. Here are some basic utensils to have on hand to make your culinary pursuits that much easier.

## Pots and Pans
- one 10" skillet with lid
- a set of covered casserole dishes
- a roasting pan with rack
- bread pans
- two cookie sheets
- double boiler
- one muffin pan with 6 to 12 cups
- Dutch oven or similar type of pan

## Gadgets
- grater
- colander
- sifter
- vegetable steamer
- food grinder
- eggbeater
- whisk
- egg slicer

## Optional Larger Gadgets
- mixer
- blender
- food processor
- toaster oven
- microwave oven
- freezer
- Crockpot

## Other Necessities
- a good set of knives
- a steel knife sharpener
- a set of measuring cups
- wooden spoons
- a mallet
- rubber spatula
- shears
- rolling pin
- storage bowls
- cheese slicer
- tongs
- garlic press

*Where's the good of putting things off?*
*Strike while the iron is hot.*

—Charles Dickens

# Quick and Easy Meal Planning

T he average woman cooks, plans, markets, chops, pares, cleans up, or eats out more than 750 meals a year! Doesn't it stand to reason that this is an area where we would need to organize? Feeding our families is certainly a big part of our lives, so here are a few easy steps and hints to make your meal planning successful.

## Keep It Simple

Fold an 8 fi" x 11" sheet of paper lengthwise in half. Fold that half cross-wise and then in half again to equal eight squares. Write the names of the days of the week in seven of the squares and "Rest" in the eighth square.

Select a main dish for each of the seven squares and plan your meals accordingly. In your planning, consider eating out, company, leftovers, and family favorites. Post your meal planner chart so all family members can see it. Should you be late arriving home, older family members can check the planner and start dinner for you. You can also list on your menu planner which person in the family is to set the table that day or week and who clears off.

| Monday | Tuesday |
|--------|---------|
| Noodle Bake | Lentil Rice Casserole |
| Wednesday | Thursday |
| Turkey Loaf | Vegetable Soup |
| Friday | Saturday |
| Pizza | Company |
| Sunday | Rest |
| Chicken Parmesan | |

# Work Your Plan

From your menu planner, make out a marketing list. I've created a shopping list where I can simply check off what items I need. List items as they appear on the aisles in your supermarket. This will prevent backtracking and spending more money. A study showed after the first half-hour in the market a woman will spend at least 75 cents per minute! You'll find you will be able to complete your shopping within 30 minutes if you stick to your list.

## ❤ Shopping List ❤

Date_____

| Qty. Staples | Qty. Drinks | Qty. Condiments | Qty. Paper Goods | Qty. Fresh Produce | Qty. Pastry |
|---|---|---|---|---|---|
| Cereal | Apple Cider | Catsup | Tissues | Fruit | Bread/s |
| Flour | Coffee | Honey | Toilet Paper | | Buns |
| Jello | Juice | Jelly/Jam | Toothpicks | | Chips |
| Mixes | Sparkling Water | Mayonnaise | Trash Bags | Vegetables | Cookies |
| Nuts | Tea | Molassas | Waxed Paper | | Crackers |
| Stuffing | | Mustard | Zip Bags | | Croutons |
| Sugar | **Canned Goods** | Oil | Small | | |
| **Spices** | Canned Fruit | Peanut Butter | Large | **Personal Items** | **Meat** |
| Bacon Bits | | Pickles | | Body Soap | Beef |
| Baking Powder | | Relish | **Household** | Deodorant | |
| Chocolate | | Salad Dressing | Bleach | Fem. Protection | Chicken |
| Coconut | | Shortening | Laundry Soap | Hair Care | |
| Salt/Pepper | Canned Meals | Syrup | Dish Soap | Makeup | |
| Soda | Canned Meat | Tomato Paste | Dishwasher Soap | | **Dairy** |
| **Pasta** | Canned Veg. | Tomato Sauce | Fabric Sofner | **Frozen Food** | Butter |
| Inst. Potato | | Vinegar | Furniture Polish | Ice Cream | Cheese |
| Mixes | | | Light Bulbs | | Cottage Cheese |
| Pasta | Soups | **Paper Goods** | Pet Food | Juice | Eggs |
| Rice | | Bacon Fool | Vacuum Bags | | Milk |
| Spaghetti | | Napkins | | | Sour Cream |
| | | Paper Towels | | TV Dinners | |
| | | Plastic Wrap | | Vegetables | |

Shop, if possible, at off hours (early morning, late evening), and shop alone. Both husbands and children can cause compromise on your list. And never shop when you're hungry, because you'll only be tempted to buy junk food.

Beware of supermarket psychology. Higher priced items are stocked at eye level. Food display at the end of aisles may appear to be on sale, but often is not.

And finally, make wise nutritional choices. Instead of ground beef, use ground turkey; darker leaf lettuce instead of light; fresh vegetables in season instead of canned or frozen; whole grain breads instead of white. Study and read labels so you're aware of additives (such as M.S.G.), preservatives, fat content, sodium, etc. Ingredients are listed in descending order by prominence of weight. The first items listed are the main ingredients in the product.

## Other Helpful Hints

- Don't forget Tupper Suppers—premade meals that are stored in Tupperware or containers in the freezer or refrigerator.

- To speed up baking potatoes, simply put a clean nail through the potato. It will cook in half the time.

- Leftover pancakes or waffles? Don't discard them; freeze them. Then pop them into the toaster or oven for a quick and easy breakfast or afterschool snack.

- Freeze lunchbox sandwiches. They can be made up by the week. Put on all the ingredients except lettuce. It will save time and trouble.

*TEN BENEFITS OF MEAL PLANNING*

*1. Saves you time*

*2. Saves you money*

*3. Saves you stress*

*4. Prevents making bad choices*

*5. Gives you better nutrition*

*6. Makes happy homes*

*7. Makes happy meals*

*8. Makes happy children*

*9. Makes happy husbands*

*10. Makes a very happy mom who has a very happy family!*

No need to boil those lasagna noodles anymore! Just spread sauce in the bottom of the pan, place hard, uncooked noodles on top and spread sauce on top of noodles. Continue with the other layers, finishing with noodles and sauce. Cover with foil and bake at 350° for 1 hour and 15 minutes.

Before freezing bagels, cut them in half. When you're ready to use them, they will defrost faster and can even be toasted while they are still frozen.

Fruit prepared ahead of time will keep well if you squeeze lemon juice over it and refrigerate. The juice of half a lemon is enough for up to two quarts of cut fruit.

By spending a little time preparing your food and planning your meals, you'll save even more time for the other things you need to do!

True happiness comes to him who does
his work well, followed by a releasing
and refreshing period of rest.

—Lin Yutang

# Setting Up a Desk and Work Area

As I began to get my home in order and to eliminate all the clutter, I soon realized that I didn't have an area to handle all the mail and paper that came into our home. It wasn't easy to follow our motto, "Don't put it down, put it away." We had piles of paper stacked in no organized fashion.

We soon realized we needed a central desk or work area in order to function properly with maximum effectiveness. Paper handling depends on a good physical setup in a practical location furnished with a comfortable working surface and a good inventory of supplies. Ideally, this office will become a permanent fixture where the business procedures of your home are done. The area should have access to supplies and files and be located where other household operations do not interfere. However, if your desk/work area can't be this ideal, don't let it stop you from getting started.

Since a desk or work area is so basic to a smoothly functioning lifestyle, here are some practical steps for setting up this area in your home.

## Choosing the Location

In order to help you choose that ideal setting, you might ask yourself these questions:

✐ Do you need to be in a place where it's quiet, or is it better for you to be near people?

✐ Do big windows distract you, or do you like being near windows?

✐ Do you prefer a sunny room or a shaded one?

✐ Do you prefer to work in the morning or in the afternoon?

The answer to these questions helps narrow your alternatives. Walk around your home to see which areas meet the answers to your four questions. After selecting at least two locations, you might ask yourself another set of questions:

✐ Is there enough space for your computer?

✐ Are there enough electrical outlets and telephone jacks?

✐ Is there enough space for a desk?

✐ Is this location out of the way of other household functions? If not, can they be shifted so they won't interfere with your office hours?

Again, add the answers to these questions to your previously selected alternatives and narrow them down to a final selection. Do you feel good about this selection? Live with it a few days before making a final decision.

## Selection of Desk, Equipment, and Supplies

After you have selected the location for your office, you need to take a sheet of paper and make a diagram of the floor plan. You will use this information when you want to make or select furniture for your new work area.

# The Desk

- *Writing surface:* Your desk should be sturdy and comfortable to use, with a surface that doesn't wobble.

- *Place for supplies:* Have at least one large drawer in which paper and envelopes can be kept in folders. If you find a desk with large drawers on each side, so much the better. There needs to be a shallow drawer with compartments for paper clips, rubber bands, and other supplies. At your local stationery store you can purchase small trays with dividers that can store these small items.

- *Files and records:* A home office seldom has need for more than one file drawer. If your desk has at least one drawer big enough to contain letter-size folders (legal-size is preferable), all your files will probably be comfortably accommodated.

- *Typing platform:* If you have a typewriter or a personal computer and plan to use it in your work area, try to get a desk with a built-in platform for these to rest on. If you have enough room in your office, you might want to designate a separate area in your office for typing and computer work.

# Other Storage Ideas

- Wall organizers are helpful for pads, pens, calendars, and other supplies.

- Paper, pencils, and supplies can be kept in stackable plastic or vinyl storage cubes under the desk.

- Use an extra bookcase shelf to store a portable typewriter, basket of supplies, or some files.

- Use stackable plastic bins that can be added to for your expanded needs. Use the small style for stationery and papers, and a larger size (a vegetable bin) for magazines and newspapers.

## Supplies

- Address book or Rolodex—I personally like both. The address book I take with me when traveling or on business, and I keep a Rolodex permanently housed on my desk. The Rolodex also has more room for adding other information you might want to use when addressing that particular person/business.

- Appointment calendar—Ideally the calendar should be small enough to carry around, as well as for use at your desk. If you search around, you can find a combination notebook and calendar that isn't too bulky to carry around in your briefcase or handbag. The date squares should be large enough to list appointments comfortably.

- Bulletin board—This is a good place to collect notes and reminders to yourself.

Decorative objects such as a ceramic mug look attractive holding pencils and pens.

- Business cards—a must time-saver

- Desk lamp

- Dictionary

- File folders—I use colored "third-cut" folders in which the stick-up tabs are staggered so they don't block each other from view. The colors give a more attractive appearance to your file drawer.

- Letter opener

- Marking pens—It is useful to have on hand a few marking pens in different colors. I do a lot of color-coding on my calendar. I also use a yellow highlighter pen when I want some information to pop out at me for rereading.

- Paper clips

- Postcards—save money on your mailing

- Pencil sharpener

- Pencils and pens

- Postage scale—a small, inexpensive type

- Rubber bands—mixed sizes

- Rubber stamp and ink pad—There are all kinds of rubber stamps you can use in your office. These are much cheaper than printed stationery or labels. If you use a certain one over and over, you might consider having a self-inking stamp made for you—it's a great time-saver.

- Ruler

- Scissors

- Scratch paper—Use lined pads for this. 3-M "Post-It Notes" are also great.

- Scotch tape and dispenser.

- Stamps—In addition to regular stamps, keep appropriate postage on hand for additional weight and special handling if you do these types of mailings regularly.

- Stapler, staples, staple remover

- Stationery and envelopes—Usually the 8-1/2" x 11" plain white paper with matching business-size envelopes is all you will need. I find 9" x 6" and 9" x 12" manila envelopes are good for mailing bulk documents, books, or magazines. Sometimes a #6 Jiffy padded envelope is useful to ship items that need some protection from rough handling in transit.

- Telephone—An extension right at your desk is great. I use my cordless telephone for this, and it works just fine.

You now have an office space that can function to meet your maximum needs. This addition to your lifestyle should certainly make you more efficient in other areas of your life. It will give you a feeling of accomplishment.

# How to Manage Your Mail

**M**ost of us can't wait for the mail to come each day, but often the thought of processing it all is overwhelming. I've discovered three easy steps that have helped me manage my mountains of mail. I hope they work for you, too!

1. *Designate one area where you open and process all your mail.* It could be a desk, a table by a chair, or the kitchen counter. If you use the kitchen counter, however, be careful not to use it as a catchall. Have a recycle bin or trash can nearby.

2. *Don't let it pile up!* Set a time each day (and I stress the each day) when you process your mail. If you can't get to it when you receive your mail, then plan a time when you can.

3. *Make decisions.* Don't put it down; put it away. And don't be a mail scooter. It's easy to scoot mail from one area to another, one room to the next, or from one pile to another. Sort out your mail into categories:

✉ *Throwaway mail*—junk mail, advertisements, etc. Junk mail is a time waster, so toss it! Don't let yourself say, "I'll probably use this someday," because you very likely will *not*.

✒ *Mail you need to read,* but don't have time for now. I slip mail such as newsletters and magazines into a file folder and take the file folder along with me in the car. When I have to wait, in the doctor's office, for children, or even in a long line, I use that time to catch up on my mail reading.

✒ *Mail you need to file away,* such as bills, insurance papers, and receipts.

✒ *Mail you need to ask someone about*—husband, children, etc. Make notes or questions marks so both of you can discuss it.

✒ *Mail that needs action.* Sometimes you have a question or need a clearer explanation than the letter gave, or you receive an address change that needs to be noted. Sort such mail together and plan a time to work through it.

✒ *Mail to be answered*—personal letters, forms to be filled out and returned, RSVPs for invitations. As a common courtesy to your host, an RSVP should be answered as soon as you know your plans. Mark dates on your calendar when the invitations arrive.

All these categories can be labeled on file folders and put into a file box or metal file cabinet. As soon as the mail comes in, simply slip it into its proper place.

Your mail *can* be managed! This is one of the easiest (and most rewarding) steps to a simply organized life.

*Personal mail goes to the person. When the children were home, all personal mail went into the folder of each individual member of the Barnes family and went directly to the person's work station. This might be a desk, a kitchen table, or his or her bed. This way we all could find our daily mail.*

# Don't Be a Paperwork Slave

Every day we make decisions about paper—from personal mail to children's schoolwork, newspapers to magazines, receipts to warranties. If you find yourself buried in years of collected, often-forgotten papers, there's hope! I have six simple steps to free you from the slavery of paperwork.

1. *Schedule set times* for sorting through papers. Doing a little each day will help to ward off paper chaos.
2. *Collect materials* you will need to help you get organized.

   - metal file cabinet or file boxes
   - plastic trash bags
   - file folders
   - black felt marking pen

3. *Start with whatever room annoys you the most.* Work your way through every pile of paper. Go through closets and drawers. When you finish a room, move on to the next.
4. *Throw away.*

   - Be determined. Make decisions. Throw away the clutter.

*Don't pile it— file it!*

&#x261E; Perhaps you have lots of articles, recipes, or children's school papers and artwork which you have been saving for that special "someday." In each category, choose five pieces to keep and get rid of the rest! Try not to be too sentimental.

&#x261E; Keep the saving of papers to a minimum. Put the throwaway papers into bags and carry them out to the trash. Don't wait. It's a good feeling!

&#x261E; Don't get bogged down rereading old letters, recipes, articles, etc. It's easy to spend too much time reminiscing and get sidetracked from your purpose of streamlining your paper-filing system.

&#x261E; Keep legal papers a minimum of seven years.

&#x261E; If you have trouble determining what to throw away, ask a friend to help you make some of those decisions. Friends tend to be more objective, and you can return the favor when they decide to simply organize.

5. *File.*

&#x261E; Categorize the papers you want to save (for example, magazine articles, family information, IRS papers, bank statements/canceled checks, charge accounts, utilities, taxes, house, and investment).

&#x261E; Within each category, mark a folder or envelope for each separate account. In the utilities, for example, you would have water, gas, electric, and the telephone. In the insurance folder it is helpful to designate separate envelopes for life, health, car, and house insurance.

 Label a folder for each member of the family. These can be used for keeping health records, report cards, notes, drawings, awards, and other special remembrances.

 Other suggestions for categories: vacation possibilities, Christmas card lists, home improvement ideas, warranties, instruction booklets, photos/negatives, and car/home repair receipts.

 File papers at the time they are received.

 Place files in cabinet or boxes.

6. *Store.*

 Store files in a closet, garage, attic, or some other area that is out of sight yet easily accessible.

 Be sure to label the file boxes. If you have set up the storage system I talked about in earlier chapters, you can note on your 3" x 5" cards the contents of each box.

You can be free from the piles of paperwork cluttering your house! Take these simple steps and start today.

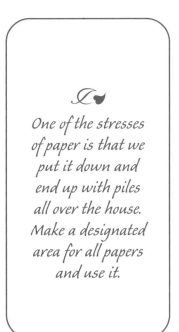

*One of the stresses of paper is that we put it down and end up with piles all over the house. Make a designated area for all papers and use it.*

Next to the dog, the
wastebasket is man's
best friend.

—Unknown

# Shortcuts to Sanity

Through the years I've collected hundreds of helpful hints to make your home more organized and your life a little easier. On the following pages you'll find some of my favorite ideas and charts to ease you through every busy day. (See page 96 for information on how you can order these forms.)

## Group Your Shopping Trips Together

In your daily planner keep a list of items you need to buy: books, videos, Christmas gifts, clothes, cosmetics, housewares, birthday and anniversary gifts. When you see a sale or go to an outlet store, you can acquire what's on your list. This will save time and a lot of money later.

## Purchase More Than One Like Item

If you have frequent demands for items like toiletries, pens, rulers, tape, and scissors, store several of each in strategic spots around the house. Don't waste time running all over the house to obtain a basic item.

## Plan on Doing More Than One Thing at a Time

Most women can do more than one thing at a time very easily with a little training. Using a cordless phone, I can do any number of things while talking to a friend or relative. I often carry along a few notecards while I'm running errands so I can write a friend if I find myself waiting for something. If you're into exercise and you have an indoor exercise machine, this is a great time to read your favorite book as you work out on your treadmill.

## Use Your Body Clock

Each of us operates most efficiently at a certain time of day. Schedule taxing chores for the hours when your mind is sharpest. Do these chores when you have the most energy.

## Store Your Keys and Glasses in One Area

My Bob used to always waste time looking for the car keys and his glasses. One day I put up a decorative key hook by the phone in the kitchen and told him to put his car keys on the hook and to place his glasses on the counter underneath the keys. Done deal—no more problem.

## Have It Picked Up and Delivered

We're returning to the good old days. More and more companies are offering these services. They are a valuable time-saver, and in many situations they are cost-efficient.

## Become a List Maker

In my daily planner I have a list for almost everything I do—from planning a tea for a group of friends to planning a Christmas party for 75 people. I save these notes so next time I can go back and review my comments. It's a great way to start planning since you already have a good beginning.

## Plan Your Errands

Do the whole group at one time. My Bob is the greatest at this. I'm continually amazed at how much he gets accomplished when he leaves to run errands. He has his list in hand, with the order of his stops. Within a short time he's back and I'm throughly impressed.

## Stop Procrastinating

Start the engine and get in motion. Even if all your ducks aren't lined up, get moving. A car has to be moving in order for it to go somewhere. Start now!

## It Doesn't Have to Be Perfect

This goes hand in hand with procrastination—not wanting to do something if it's not perfect. It's nice to want things done right, but not if you are crippled into inactivity. You may know the difference, but your friends and guests won't know it's not perfect. Some jobs don't need perfection. Just do it.

## Shop Once for Greeting Cards

Rather than going out 15 or 20 times during the year, I spend 30 minutes to an hour once or twice a year at a card shop. I take the sheet labeled "Dates and Occasions" to help me pick out the cards for everyone that I'm going to need to send a card to throughout the year. Along with that I'll add some anniversary cards, get-well cards, and sympathy cards. Then I file all the cards in file folders marked "Greeting Cards."

## The Gift Shelf

Somewhere in your home it's nice to have a gift shelf. At any of the department store sales, pick up a few nice items—a box of stationery, little teddy bears, or whatever is useful. I've always had a gift shelf in my home. When the children had a birthday party to go to, I would let them go pick out what they wanted from the shelf to give to Bradley Joe or Weston or whomever. This way you've got something right there, and you don't have to run out to a department store, spending a lot of time and money.

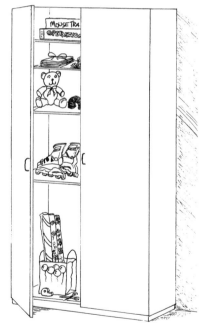

## The Gift Wrap Shelf

It saves time and money to have a gift wrap shelf (or box or drawer). Once a year I'll go to where they have gift wrap on sale.

On your gift wrap shelf you should have some colored ribbon, Scotch tape, and a few dried or silk flowers to put on a package. You should also have some mailing labels and strapping tape.

*There is a time for everything,*

*and a season for every*

*activity under heaven.*

*—The Book of Ecclesiastes*

# The Family History Chart

Here you can list your children's names, their birth dates, their blood types, dates of their yearly physical, their dental exams, their eye exams, when they had their inoculations, etc. Everything is nicely listed here so you can refer back to it.

### ✍❤ Family History ✍❤

| Family Member Name | Birth Date | Blood Type | Date of Last: | | | Inoculation Date | Other |
|---|---|---|---|---|---|---|---|
| | | | Yearly Physical | Dental Exam | Eye Exam | | |
| | | | | | | | |
| | | | | | | | |
| | | | | | | | |
| | | | | | | | |
| | | | | | | | |
| | | | | | | | |
| | | | | | | | |
| | | | | | | | |
| | | | | | | | |
| | | | | | | | |
| | | | | | | | |
| | | | | | | | |
| | | | | | | | |
| | | | | | | | |

# Shopping Guide Chart

The family Shopping Guide Chart is a practical way of knowing how your family grows. This will enable you to quickly give grandparents and family members children's clothing sizes.

## ✍❤ Shopping Guide ✍❤

| Family Member Name | SIZES | | | | | Favorite Activities | Other Clubs Interests, Etc. |
|---|---|---|---|---|---|---|---|
| | Dress/Suit | Shoes | Pants | Socks | Underwear | | |
| | | | | | | | |
| | | | | | | | |
| | | | | | | | |
| | | | | | | | |
| | | | | | | | |
| | | | | | | | |
| | | | | | | | |
| | | | | | | | |
| | | | | | | | |
| | | | | | | | |
| | | | | | | | |
| | | | | | | | |
| | | | | | | | |
| | | | | | | | |
| | | | | | | | |
| | | | | | | | |

# The Credit Cards Sheet

List the name of the company, the account number, the address, the telephone number, and when the card expires. Then, if it's lost or stolen, you can quickly go to your notebook and report it immediately. If you do some purchasing over the telephone, you have the number handy, and you won't have to fumble through your purse trying to find your credit card.

## ❧ Credit Cards ❧

| Company | Card Number | Company Address | Company Phone Number | Card Expires (Date) |
|---------|-------------|-----------------|----------------------|---------------------|
|  |  |  |  |  |
|  |  |  |  |  |
|  |  |  |  |  |
|  |  |  |  |  |
|  |  |  |  |  |
|  |  |  |  |  |
|  |  |  |  |  |
|  |  |  |  |  |
|  |  |  |  |  |
|  |  |  |  |  |
|  |  |  |  |  |
|  |  |  |  |  |
|  |  |  |  |  |
|  |  |  |  |  |
|  |  |  |  |  |

# The Important Numbers Sheet

List phone numbers for the police, the fire department, the ambulance service, the poison control service, the neighbors, etc.

## ✿ Important Numbers ✿

| Service Person | Phone Number | Service Person | Phone Number |
|---|---|---|---|
| Ambulance | | Neighbor | |
| Appliance Repair | | Newspaper | |
| Dentist | | Orthodontist | |
| Doctor | | Pastor | |
| Electrician | | Poison Control | |
| Fire | | Police | |
| Gardener | | Pool Service | |
| Gas Co. Emergency | | Plumber | |
| Glass Repair | | School(s) | |
| Heating/Air Conditioning Repair Person | | School(s) | |
| Husband's Work | | Veterinarian | |
| Insurance (Car) | | Cat's Name | |
| Insurance (Home) | | Dog's Name | |

# Dates and Occasions

List everybody's birthday, everybody's anniversary, and all the other important dates for the year. As each month comes up, check to see whose birthday is listed. You can show on the chart if you sent a card or what kind of gift you gave last year.

## ❧ Dates and Occasions ❧

| Month | Date/Occasion | Name of Person(s) | Gift(s) Given | Month | Date/Occasion | Name of Person(s) | Gift(s) Given |
|---|---|---|---|---|---|---|---|
| January | | | | July | | | |
| February | | | | August | | | |
| March | | | | September | | | |
| April | | | | October | | | |
| May | | | | November | | | |
| June | | | | December | | | |

# The Home Instructions Sheet

The next time you have someone housesit or take care of your children while you're away, leave a Home Instructions Sheet. You can note your weekly routine as well as things like trash pick up. Maybe your mother-in-law sees this man walking around in your backyard one day, and she doesn't know who he is. She can check the Home Instructions Sheet and say, "That's the pool man, or that's the gardener, so I'm not going to worry about him."

### ✍ Home Instructions ✍

| | Routine Chores/Errands | Special Appointments |
|---|---|---|
| Sunday | | |
| Monday | | |
| Tuesday | | |
| Wednesday | | |
| Thursday | | |
| Friday | | |
| Saturday | | |

# The Items Loaned List

For many years I loaned items to my friends, thinking I would surely remember who had my turkey platter, Tupperware bowls, picnic basket, and the children's sleeping bags. You know what? I forgot after a short period of time! This simple form makes it easy to keep track of what you've loaned.

## ✑❤ Items Loaned List ✑❤

Month/Year

| Date | Item | Who | Returned |
|------|------|-----|----------|
|      |      |     |          |
|      |      |     |          |
|      |      |     |          |
|      |      |     |          |
|      |      |     |          |
|      |      |     |          |
|      |      |     |          |
|      |      |     |          |
|      |      |     |          |
|      |      |     |          |
|      |      |     |          |
|      |      |     |          |
|      |      |     |          |
|      |      |     |          |
|      |      |     |          |
|      |      |     |          |
|      |      |     |          |
|      |      |     |          |

# The On Order List

Have you ever forgotten what you've ordered from your favorite catalog? Or which manufacturer's rebate coupons you have sent in? Spend a few minutes recording those "on-order" items that need to be tracked until they have been received.

### ✒♥ On Order List ✒♥

| Date Ordered | Item | Company | Date Due | Received |
|---|---|---|---|---|
| | | | | |
| | | | | |
| | | | | |
| | | | | |
| | | | | |
| | | | | |
| | | | | |
| | | | | |
| | | | | |
| | | | | |
| | | | | |
| | | | | |
| | | | | |
| | | | | |
| | | | | |
| | | | | |
| | | | | |

# Love Baskets

One of the joys of a simply organized life is having time to do the special things you *want* to do. For me, creating little surprises for the people in my life who I love is something I *now* have time for. One of my favorite treats is what I call "Love Basket". It can be filled with food for dinner at the beach, or it can be taken to a ball game. It can *even* be taken in your car on a love trip. It may be a surprise lunch or dinner in the backyard, in your bedroom, or under a tree, but be creative and use it to say "I love you."

## What You'll Need

Here are the things you'll need in order to make a Love Basket. First of all, you'll need a basket with a handle, preferably a heavy-duty basket something like a picnic basket without a lid. Then you'll need a tablecloth, about 45" square. You'll want to line the inside of your basket with this tablecloth, letting it drape over the sides so it looks real cute. I make these for wedding shower gifts, anniversary gifts, or bridal gifts.

Inside the basket put two fancy glasses with stems. You'll also need four napkins. I like to use one with a small print, or maybe a gingham, to make the basket look fun and different. One napkin will be for the lap and the other will be used as a napkin, but for now fluff up your napkins inside the top of the glasses so they puff up and look like powder puffs inside your glasses.

Next you'll need to add a nice tall candle holder and a candle. I like to use something tall because it shows over the top of the basket. You'll also need a bottle of sparkling apple cider. You'll want a loaf of French bread, plus some pretty fresh flowers to make the basket look fun and inviting. Also, you'll want some cheese, salami, dill pickles, and any other good things that you really like.

I've been making Love Baskets for my husband for more than 40 years. We all sense times when our husband needs a little extra attention. Maybe things have been tough at work, or maybe he's depressed over something, or maybe he just needs to feel that he's needed. These are times when you want to put together a Love Basket.

I can remember saying to a friend or neighbor, "You know, my Bob needs a Love Basket tomorrow night, and I'd like to do it for him. Would you take the kids for a few hours for me? The next time your husband needs a Love Basket, I'll take your kids for you." I tell you, they're happy to do it for you. And I'm happy to do it for anyone.

One Valentine's Day Bob and I weren't going to be able to be together, so I decided I would make a Love Basket for him the night before. That morning I called him at work and said, "Tonight I want to take you out to a special restaurant that you've never been to before that has your very favorite food." He asked, "Well, where is it?" I replied, "I'm not going to tell you. It's just a special place in town that I'm going to take you tonight. Could you be home by six o'clock?" Do you know what? He got home at 5:30!

What he didn't know was that during the morning I had fried his very favorite Southern fried chicken. I had also made potato salad, fruit salad, and some yummy rolls. I had the whole dinner prepared in the morning because I didn't want the house to smell from food and give away the surprise when he walked in the door that night.

Love Baskets add a special touch to any occasion—and they're simple to do.

# Simply Organized . . .

# Especially for Kids

*He that riseth late must*
*trot all day.*

—Ben Franklin

# Children Need to Be Organized, Too

When my children were young, I can honestly say that their ideas and my ideas of organization were completely different—like North Pole and South Pole! There were a few ideas that did work, though, and I'm sure they'll work for you. (I'm also happy to report that both my children, now grown, are more organized than I am in some areas!)

## The Children's File Box

When our children were about 12 or 13 years old, I set up a file box for each of them. (I wish I had done it even earlier). I gave them ten file folders, and one day we went through their rooms and organized. They began to file all their report cards, all their special reports, and all their pictures and letters. Jenny was lucky enough to get some love letters, so she filed those in her file box. She also pressed and filed the flowers from her special dates and proms. When she got her first car, the insurance papers all went into the file box.

When the children went away to college, the first thing they took with them was their file box. It had all their important papers. When they came home for the summer, home came the file box. When Jenny was married, she took her file box with her. All her little treasures were in that box. Then she got another box and ten more file folders, and she set up a household file box. So now she has all those warranties, instruction booklets, and insurance papers in her household file.

## Other Great Ideas for Organizing the Kids

- Keep those socks sorted by pinning them together with a safety pin or clipping them together with clothespins. Put the child's initials on the socks with a black paint pen.

- Review the family calendar together. On Sunday evening we would go over our large desktop calendar to see where we were all going to be during the coming week. Were there any transportation or babysitting needs—any church activities, birthday parties, holidays, etc.? Is all homework ready for Monday at school? Any gifts needed for the week? This lets us touch bases and make sure we were all on the same schedule.

- Have one area where the children place all their school items. I used colored bins by the front door where each child would put his/her gym clothes, homework, schoolbooks. This saved a lot of last-minute hunting for items before running off to school.

- Have a dress-up box available for those spontaneous plays that your children perform on days they play inside because of weather. Today I use these old clothes for the grandchildren when they come over to play.

- Have a box of games, toys, and coloring books to take with you on long trips. Also bring along an old sheet and spread it on the back seat and floor. Let all the debris fall on the sheet. When you get to your destination, all you have to do is pull out the sheet, shake it on the ground, and put it back in the car.

- Color-code your children. Jenny knew that the yellow towels were hers, and Brad knew that his were blue.

- Make sure that each child has a place to hang clothes and store belongings. This place doesn't have to be expensive. Many times plastic bins and wooden crates work fine.

- Put the van Gogh artwork of your young artist on the refrigerator, bulletin board, or in a folder designated for that child's age or grade in school. Some of the extra artwork can be used in wrapping grandparents' gifts.

- Clean out a bedroom before the arrival of new items. Before birthdays, Christmas, and the change of seasons, go through the bedroom with the child assisting and help clean out old clothes, broken toys, and clothes that are too small. Be sure to use my three-bag system: 1) Give Away, 2) Put Away, and 3) Throw Away. Give obsolete items to friends, neighbors, or charities.

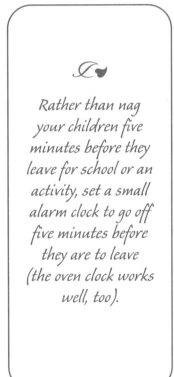

*Rather than nag your children five minutes before they leave for school or an activity, set a small alarm clock to go off five minutes before they are to leave (the oven clock works well, too).*

- Children need shelves, hooks, and bins. Let the children help decide where these items should be placed in the room.

- Each room needs a bulletin board to store all those pictures, awards, certificates, postcards, and special items.

- Each child needs to have a study center. Make sure there is plenty of light, basic supplies of pencils, pens, paper, paper clips, a stapler, ruler, hole punch, rubber bands. If this isn't possible, put all these items into a color-coded plastic bin.

- At least once a month set aside a special afternoon where the children are invited to the kitchen to prepare a meal or a portion of a meal. Desserts are always a winner. Bring out the aprons and chef's hat—if they dress like cooks, they will really get involved in the process.

- I have an old cowbell that is positioned by our kitchen door. Two minutes before a meal I go out and ring that bell very firmly. This is a signal to the members of the family that the food is ready. They have two minutes to get to the table.

- Children get bored of doing the same chores all the time. Rotate them periodically.

# Jobs for Kids

Delegating responsibility to children is such an important aspect of motherhood that you should be giving your children responsibilities at a very young age. Make it fun for them; make games out of it. A three-year-old can dress himself, put his pajamas away, brush his hair, brush his teeth, and make his bed. You can begin to teach your children these things when they're as young as two and three years old. Some more examples: folding clothes, emptying the dishwasher, clearing some of the dishes off the table, emptying wastebaskets, or picking up toys before bedtime (plastic baskets are excellent for toys).

It is our responsibility as parents to train our children and direct them and guide them in the ways that they should go, so that when they become adults they're not domestic invalids. It's important that we give our children responsibilities and train them up. As you go through your home, take your little one with you and begin to show him what you're doing. Often children don't even realize that there's toothpaste on the mirror in the bathroom because they've never been told that they have to wipe it up. They think it just somehow automatically disappears.

Here are some more things children can do:

## Three-year-old
1. Get dressed, put pajamas away
2. Brush hair
3. Brush teeth

4. Make bed
5. Fold clothes and small items
6. Empty dishwasher (will need help with this)
7. Clear meal dishes
8. Empty wastebaskets
9. Pick up toys before bed

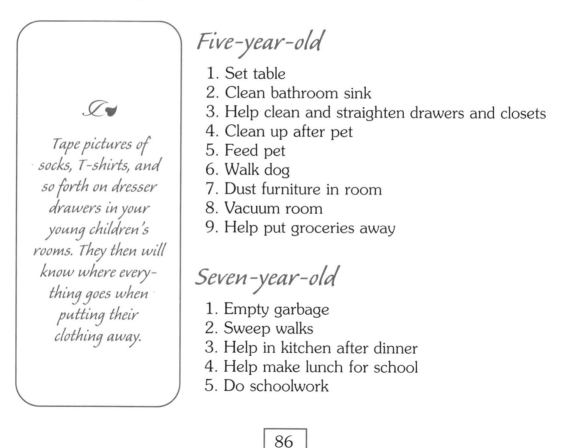

*Tape pictures of socks, T-shirts, and so forth on dresser drawers in your young children's rooms. They then will know where everything goes when putting their clothing away.*

## Five-year-old

1. Set table
2. Clean bathroom sink
3. Help clean and straighten drawers and closets
4. Clean up after pet
5. Feed pet
6. Walk dog
7. Dust furniture in room
8. Vacuum room
9. Help put groceries away

## Seven-year-old

1. Empty garbage
2. Sweep walks
3. Help in kitchen after dinner
4. Help make lunch for school
5. Do schoolwork

6. Clean out car
7. Iron flat items

## Eight-year-old

1. Wash bathroom mirrors
2. Wash windows
3. Wash floors in small area
4. Polish shoes

As your children grow, more responsibility can be given to them:

1. Wash car
2. Mow lawn
3. Make dessert
4. Paint
5. Clean refrigerator
6. Do yard work
7. Iron
8. Fix an entire meal
9. Do grocery shopping

We cannot do it all by ourselves in our homes (when we try, we become frustrated). When we begin to delegate responsibilities to our children and allow them to do some of the work for us, they begin to feel as if they are a vital part of the family.

# The Laundry Game

Take a piece of fabric (a remnant or whatever—something with a lot of color in it) and make a laundry bag about 20 inches wide by 36 inches high. You might want to use a king-sized pillowcase with a shoelace strung through the top. Then say to your little ones, "Okay, we're going to play a game." Don't tell them it's work. By the time they're ten, they will realize you've been working them to death, but they don't know it when they're little. Say, "We're going to play a game, and it's called sort-the-laundry." Then get out your laundry bag that has lots of colors and say, "This is the bag where all the dirty clothes that have a lot of colors go. Now find something in this dirty-clothes pile that has a lot of colors." So they run over and pick it up, and you say, "Right! Now put it in the colored laundry bag." So they put it in there.

Then make a bag that is navy blue or dark brown and tell them, "This is where all the dark-colored clothes go." This would be the blue jeans, the brown T-shirts, the navy-blue socks—all those dark-colored clothes. "Now run over and find something that's dark-colored." You see, you're playing a game with them. They do it, and you say, "Great! That's absolutely right!"

Then you make a bag that's all white, and you say, "Now this is where the white dirty clothes go—the white T-shirts, the white socks, the white underwear. They go into the white laundry bag."

Now you're going to give them a little test. You say, "Okay, now find me something that's colored." They run over and pick it up. And then, "Find something that's white." And they put it into the proper bag. What you're doing now is actually teaching children as young as four years old how to sort the laundry.

## Bags and More Bags

Another thing I did that really worked out well was to make individual laundry bags for each of the kids to hang in their room behind their door or in their closet. This is where they put their own dirty clothes. Then whoever's job it was for the week to sort the laundry merely went around, collected everybody's laundry bag, and sorted these into three large laundry bags I had by my washing machine.

One gal gave me a great idea, which I think is fantastic if you have the room. Go out and buy three of those plastic trash cans in different colors, and put them in the garage. You can label them white clothes, dark clothes, and colored clothes with a felt-tip pen. Then your kids can sort the clothes by playing a basketball game with the clothes and trying to hit the right containers.

## The Chore Basket

Take a good look at the Daily Work Planner Chart. What we would do was to take all the chores for the

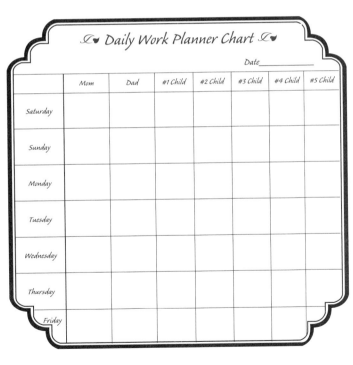

Daily Work Planner Chart

Date_____

| | Mom | Dad | #1 Child | #2 Child | #3 Child | #4 Child | #5 Child |
|---|---|---|---|---|---|---|---|
| Saturday | | | | | | | |
| Sunday | | | | | | | |
| Monday | | | | | | | |
| Tuesday | | | | | | | |
| Wednesday | | | | | | | |
| Thursday | | | | | | | |
| Friday | | | | | | | |

week, write them on individual pieces of paper, and put them in a basket. Then we would go around one by one and allow the children to choose—to pick out a chore. It was like a little game; whatever they chose was the chore they had to do for the week. And it would go on the Daily Work Planner Chart.

Notice that Mom and Dad are listed on the chart too. What it shows the kids is that we're working together as a family. At the end of the day, when they've checked their charts and have done their chores as best they can, you can put a little happy face on the chart. Stickers are great also. At the end of the week you can check your chart and say, "You know, our family did a fantastic job this week. We're going to have a picnic at the park (or go bicycling together, or have an evening with popcorn together, or do something else that's fun together) because we've really worked well together in accomplishing this."

If you have a wide range of ages in your home, you might want to use two baskets—one for the smaller children and one for the rest of the family. That way the little children don't draw jobs that are too difficult. It is also important that Mom and Dad inspect to make sure the chores are done properly. Remember, "It's not what you expect, but what you inspect" that teaches children to be responsible family members.

## Setting the Table

A five-year-old can learn to set the table. It amazed me when our daughter, Jenny, would bring her friends home at 16 or 17 years of age and they didn't even know how to set a table. They didn't know where a knife, fork, and spoon went. It wasn't their fault. It was because Mom or Dad never took the time to teach them. As the five-year-old sets the table you can say, "Okay, Chad, do whatever you want. You can use Mom's good china, or you can use paper plates, or you can have candlelight, or you can put your favorite teddy bear on the table. I don't care—whatever you want to do."

Too many times we put the good china on the table only for when company comes and at Christmas. Who are the most important people in our lives? Our family! And we seldom use the good china for those people who mean the very most to us. I look at it this way: We can't take the china with us, so if a piece gets broken here and there, it gets broken. I would rather have my children be able to enjoy the nicer things and to use them and live with them than to have them in a china cabinet where they can't be enjoyed. So let your children have the freedom to use the good china and teach them as you go along how to set the table.

## The Weekly Calendar

You can list those things that are going to go on for the week; you can quickly look through the calendar and see when you're going to be needed, when you're going to need to pick up so-and-so. And you can feel free now because you know where you're needed and

### ♥ Weekly Calendar ♥

|         | Monday | Tuesday | Wednesday | Thursday | Friday | Saturday | Sunday |
|---------|--------|---------|-----------|----------|--------|----------|--------|
| Morning |        |         |           |          |        |          |        |
| Noon    |        |         |           |          |        |          |        |
| Night   |        |         |           |          |        |          |        |

where your children will have to be. Check it over and fill it out the night before so you'll know what's happening the next day. Also fill in your work schedule if you work outside your home. Then your family can see it and know what's going on.

## The Bed Lesson

I asked our son after his second year in college, "Brad, do you make your bed at school?" He replied, "Mom, I'm the only one in my house who makes my bed." I know why he does it, because once when he was about eight years old he hadn't made his bed for four mornings in a row. I had let him get away with it a little now and then, but four mornings was just too much. He was halfway down the block with a couple of his little buddies when I noticed his unmade bed and went running after him. When I caught up with him I said, "Brad, I really hate to do this, but this is the fourth morning in a row you haven't made your bed. So I'm going to have to ask you to please go back in and make your bed." He replied, "Mom, you wouldn't!" I said, "Well, I'm really sorry, but I'm going to have to do it." He responded, "But I'm going to be late for school!" I came back with, "I know you're going to be late for school, but we'll worry about that later." So he came home and made his bed. Then he said, "You know I'm going to need a note for my teacher." I replied, "Fine, I'll be happy to write you a note." I wrote him a note saying that Brad was late because this was the fourth morning in a row that he had not made his bed, and that the teacher could do whatever she wanted with him. You know what? I never had any trouble with Brad making his bed after that!

## Helping Kids Come to Breakfast

We get breakfast cooked and call everyone to the table, but they don't come. Isn't that irritating? I think that was one of the things that bothered me the most. How are we going to correct this problem? I said to the children, "We're going to have a meeting." I continued, "You know, I've really got a problem. I call you children for breakfast, but you don't come. Now is there anything you might suggest that could help with this problem?" So they said to me, "Golly, Mom, if you'd just let us know a couple of minutes before breakfast is ready, we'd come right to the table." So that's what we did. You can ring a chime, play the piano, sing a song, blow a whistle—whatever you want to do. Give them a warning to let them know that breakfast or dinner is going to be ready within a few minutes, and they'll come. It absolutely worked beautifully in our family.

## Other Helpful Hints

To help children remember the proper way to set the table, tell them that fork and left both have four letters, while knife, spoon, and right all have five letters.

🖝 From a creative mother: After many nights of interrupted sleep, I finally hit on a solution that keeps my five-year-old in her bed—at least most nights. I labeled one bowl "Mama's Bed Buttons" and another "Christine's Bed Buttons" and put 25 small buttons in each. For every night Christine stays in bed, I owe her one button. She pays me a button if she gets in bed with me. When her button bowl is filled, we do something special—a roller-skating trip, a movie, an outing of her choice. Now she only comes to my bed if she really feels she has to.

❧ One most-appreciated gift a neighbor gave me after the birth of my first baby was a freshly baked apple pie with a card attached worth eight hours of free babysitting. The pie hit the spot, since I was tired of eating all the hospital food, and it was reassuring to know there was someone available close by to babysit if needed.

❧ Once a year, have a babysitter swap party. Each attendee must bring the names and telephone numbers of three reliable sitters.

❧ A tasty variation on the standard peanut-butter-and-jelly sandwich: Make the sandwich as usual, but just before serving, butter the outside of the bread, and brown the sandwich in a hot skillet.

❧ When sewing buttons on children's clothing, use elastic thread. It makes buttoning much simpler for little fingers.

❧ Here is a little idea for young children at a fast-food store or restaurant. When you buy the tot a soft drink, cut the straw off short so it is easier to hold and drink. There is less chance of a child spilling or dropping the drink, too.

❧ Put a plastic cloth under your young child's high chair. After they are finished eating, all you have to do is take the plastic outside and shake off all the crumbs.

# How to Get More Hours in Your Day

**Start Your Day the Night Before**
- Set the breakfast table the night before.
- Gather wash and sort it.
- Set up the coffeepot for morning.
- Make a list of what must be done the next day.

**Get Up Early**
- The last one out of the bed makes the bed!
- Put in the first load of wash.
- Shower and dress.

**Advance to the Kitchen**
- Rejoice that the table is set and attractive.
- Prepare breakfast.
- Call everyone to the table with a "two-minute warning."
- Have everyone take their dishes to the sink when through.
- Put all dishes in the sink to soak in hot water.
- Check your "To Do" list.

**Put Your Day in Full Swing**
- Have each child check his or her room.

- Check the bathroom for clothes and cleanliness.
- Have your children check for their lunch or money, books, homework, gym clothes, etc.

**Get Back to Work or Off to Work**
- Put in a second load of wash.
- Do the dishes.
- Do any advance dinner preparation.
- Clean up the counters.
- Rejoice that your basic housework is done!
- Check your "To Do" list.

**Prepare Your Home for the Evening**
- Prepare munchies if dinner is a bit late.
- Start to unwind and think toward a quiet, gentle spirit.
- Organize the children as best as you possibly can.
- Do not share the negative part of the day with your family until after dinner.
- Enjoy your family.

To obtain information about Emilie Barnes' seminars, tapes, and other helpful time-management products, send a self-addressed, stamped envelope to:

More Hours in My Day
2838 Rumsey Drive
Riverside, CA 92506